Seniors Sign, Too!

ASL ALPHABET BOOK #1

Empowering Older Adults with an Alternative Voice
Promoting Healthy Aging After Hearing Loss

D'YANN ELAINE, M.ED, MAOM
Illustrated in American Sign Language by Filip Heyninck

COPYRIGHT

Seniors Sign, Too! Illustrated in American Sign Language

For more information on special discounts for bulk purchases, please contact Sales at (424) 261-8502
hearzerosales@signwithme.org or visit our website: https://signwithme.org

Publisher's Cataloging-in-Publication data.

NAMES: Elaine, D'yann, author | Heyninck, Filip, illustrator

TITLE: *Seniors sign, too! ASL Alphabet illustrated in American Sign Language:
empowering older adults with an alternative voice, promoting healthy aging after hearing loss*
by D'yann Elaine; illustrated by Filip Heyninck.

SERIES: Seniors, Sign Too!

DESCRIPTION: Los Angeles, CA: D'yann Elaine, 2022.

IDENTIFIERS: LCCN: 2022907495 | ISBN: 979-8-9861021-0-8 (hardcover) |
979-8-9861021-1-5 (paperback) | 979-8-9861021-2-2 (e-Book)

SUBJECTS: LCSH American Sign Language. | Sign language--Handbooks, manuals, etc. | Older people. |
Hearing disorders. | Older deaf people. | BISAC LANGUAGE ARTS & DISCIPLINES/Sign Language. |
SELF-HELP/Aging. | FAMILY & RELATIONSHIPS/Life Stages/Later Years. | FAMILY & RELATIONSHIPS/Eldercare.

CLASSIFICATION: LCC HV2474 .D93 2022 | DDC 419--dc23

DEDICATION

I dedicate this book with love, admiration,
and gratitude for the people in my life:

To my jewel, my daughter, my inspiration, A. Brytney Reaves.

To my parents, Larry and Leeaada Dorsey,
for always loving me and teaching me how to love, and for supporting
me and choosing me against many odds. I love you eternally.

To the beautiful people of the Deaf community, with my humble
appreciation. Thank you for embracing me as an ally and entrusting
me to share your treasured language, a vivid canvas of exquisite
expressions. I am honored to support ASL awareness and stand
with you for diversity, equality and inclusion for individuals
who are Deaf and hard-of-hearing in all settings and industry.
I pray the world will see ASL for what it is: a rich and expressive
cognitive delight that unites humans, instills peace, builds
relationships, making our world a better place for all mankind.

INTRODUCTION

Welcome to the most unique and entertaining alphabet book ever! Written with the aging adult perspective in mind, this book series is the perfect way for older adults, ages 55 and up, to engage in sign language as an alternative visual communication tool. The books feature an illustrated cast of characters and a delightful interplay between letters and drawings. This combination brings nostalgic memories to mind while seamlessly connecting with today's reality.

Whether young, old, or in between, you are invited to join our HearZero community of signers. We empower older adults with a way to communicate visually when it becomes more challenging to express their thoughts with words.

Welcome

AGE
88
A

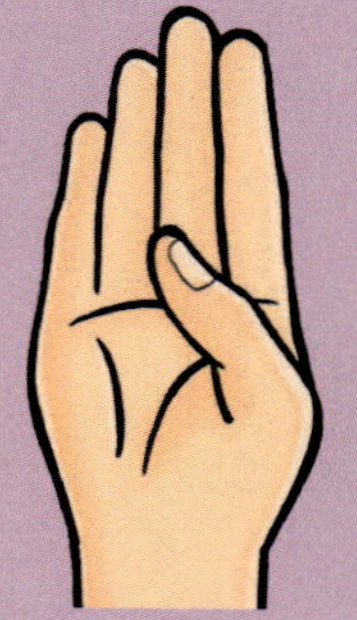

B

CONFUSE

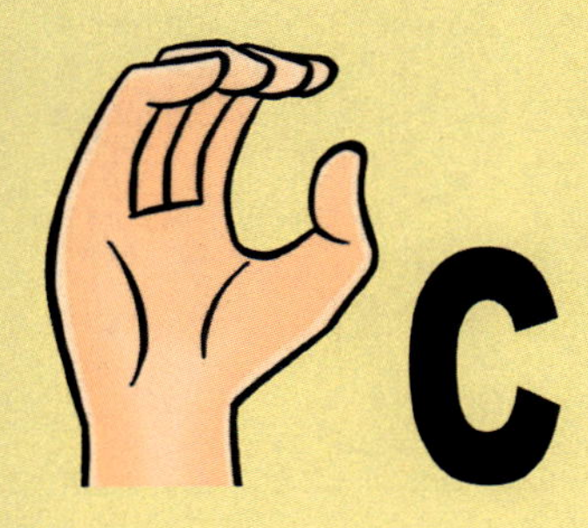

C

DOCTOR

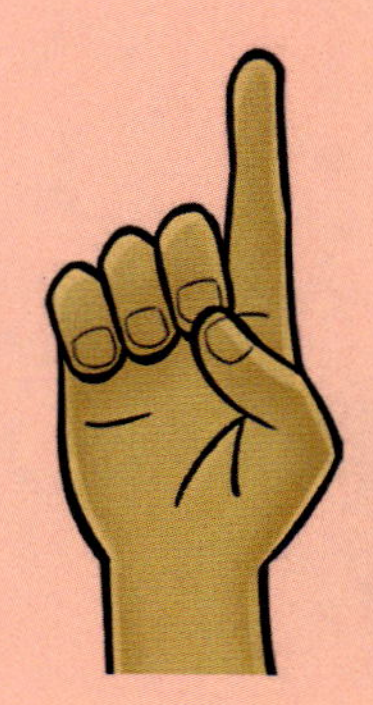

D

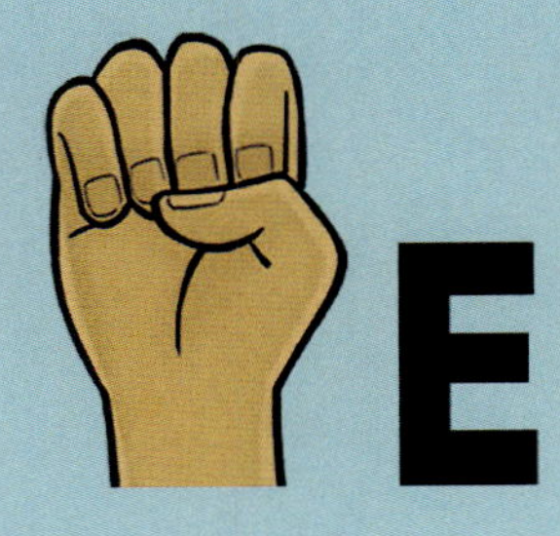

E

FOOD

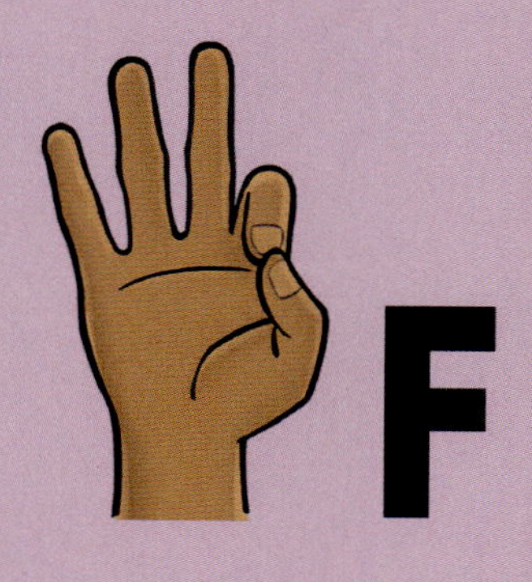
F

FAST FOOD
FRIES AND COKE
BURGER AND COFFEE
DONUTS
PIZZA AND COKE
HearZero Cafe

GIVE

HOSPITAL

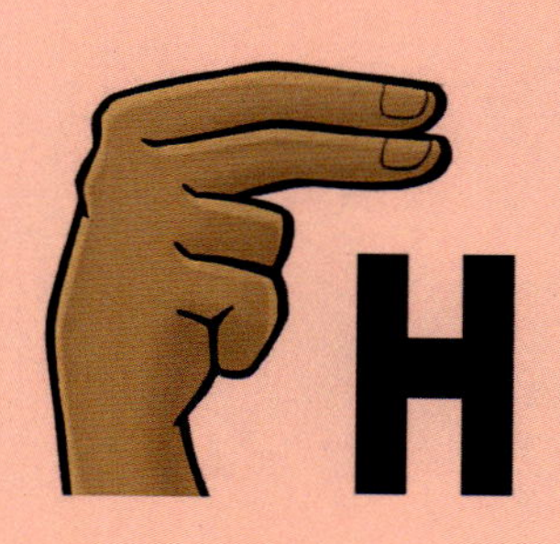

H

I / ME
I

1
2
JOIN
J

KIND

1
2
LOST
FINE DINING
LUNCH ROOM
HEARZERO CAFE ™
DINING HALL
L

MEDICINE

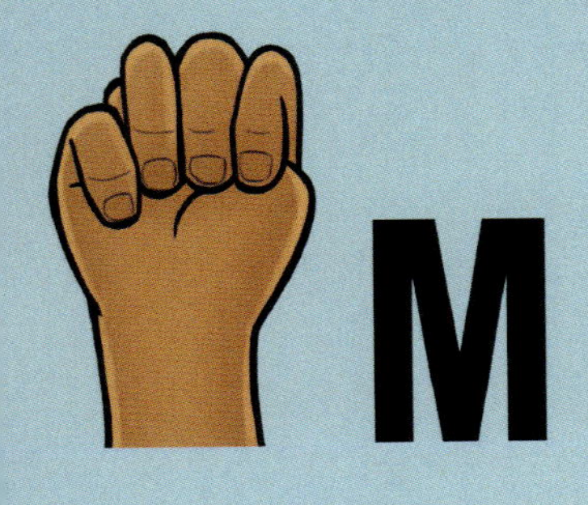
M

NURSE

N

OFF
OFF / ON
ON
O

PRIEST

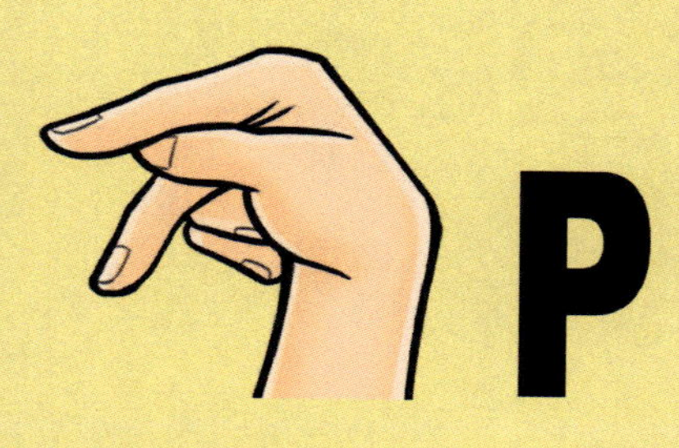

P

QUIET
Q

RESTROOM

R

STINK

S

TASTE

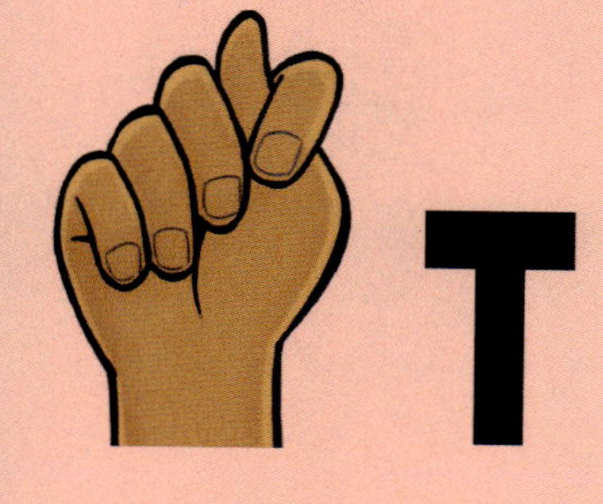

UPSET

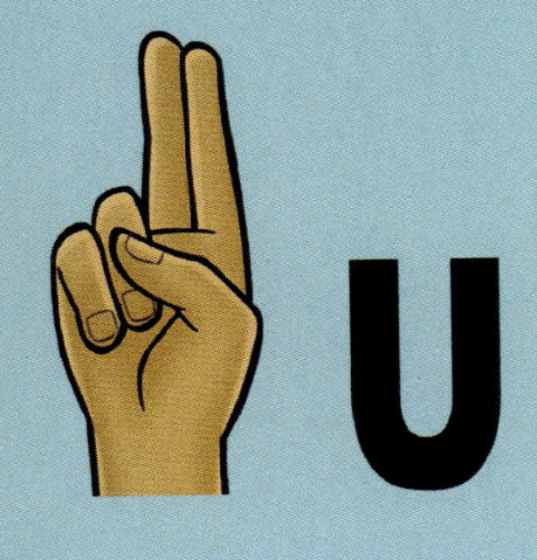

VOMIT

V

Pepto

WAIT
W
M
METRO
STOP

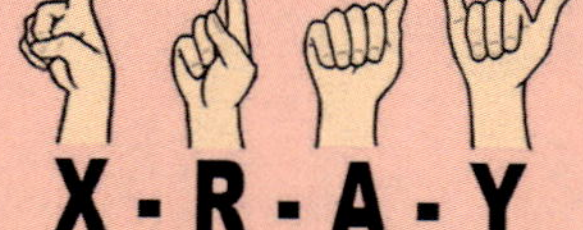
X-R-A-Y

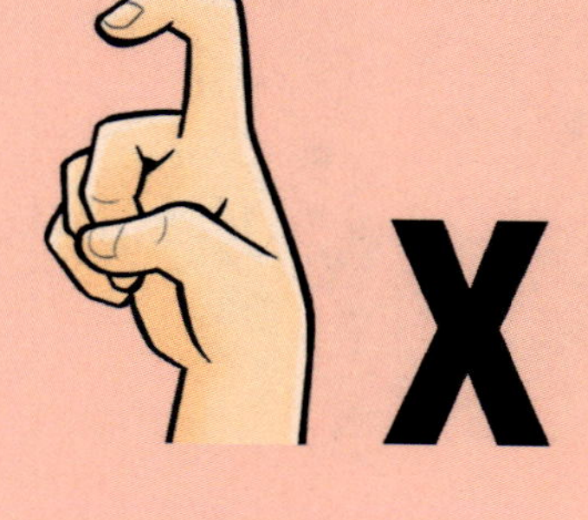
X

2 x
YES

Y

SLEEP

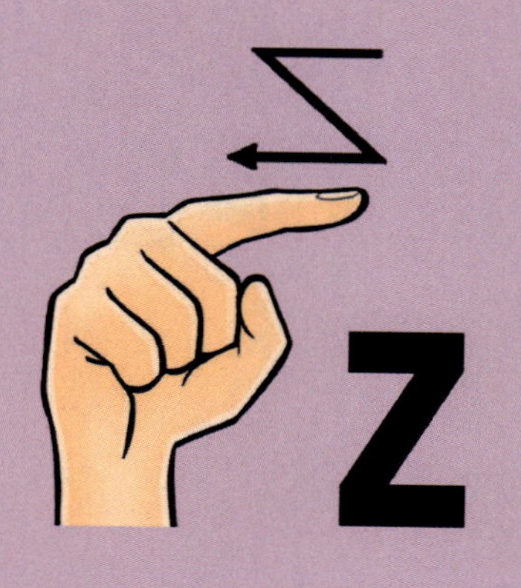

ABOUT THE AUTHOR

D'YANN ELAINE, American Sign Language (ASL) educator, interpreter, consultant, author, producer, and founder of Sign with Me, Inc., is a master architect who is able to connect the hearing and d/Deaf communities. In doing so, she trailblazes territories formerly charted by few who dare to venture.

D'YANN ELAINE, M.ED, MAOM

Born in Watts, and former USC Women of Troy basketball player, D'yann holds two Bachelors and two Masters degrees from prestigious Universities. She harnesses a force filled with passion, persistence, and a love for social equity and inclusion. D'yann's goal is to help others expand their purview beyond the lens of their inabilities—to the scope of their abilities. For more than two decades, D'yann has made her life's work teaching others. She is the executive producer of ASL Emergency Preparedness DVD Series and Unheard Voices Talk Show, as well as the author of the *Seniors Sign, Too!* book series. Her vision is to spark a whole new community of signers, and make a profound impact by unifying communities through language.

ABOUT THE ILLUSTRATOR

FILIP HEYNINCK

FILIP HEYNINCK is a renowned Deaf illustrator. He resides in Waasmunster, Belgium with his wife Katrien Van Laere, two adult hearing children (CODAs), Kimberly and Dalvin, one dog and two cats. Filip is a dedicated husband and father and an extraordinary cartoonist and illustrator. He has been drawing and creating visual artwork since he learned to hold a pencil as a toddler. His wife Katrien is a graphic designer who colors all his drawings and does the layout and administrative tasks. Together, Filip and Katrien are a dynamic duo.

Filip's works have occupied bookstore shelves since 2005, and include comic books, such as *Deaf Devils and Slim Gezien*, which inspired his own first comic book publications, *The *S.P.O.R.T.S: Gold...Set! Match!*, *Otherworldly Game*, and *Ninia Dance Battle.*

Website: http://www.filipheyninck.com, Email: filip.heyninck1@telenet.be,
Social Media: FB, IG @filipheyninck

ABOUT THE TEAM

KATHLEEN MARCATH

KATHLEEN MARCATH has a B.A. degree in Deaf Community Studies from Madonna University. She is a children's book author whose interest in ASL escalated when she learned to sign the song, *Our God Is an Awesome God*. The beauty and power of ASL captured her attention and never let go. Countless times, she has watched the same magic illuminate other people's faces (deaf and hearing alike) when they learn this beautiful language. Her goal is to promote ASL literacy and raise awareness of its importance to audiences of all ages and backgrounds. In 2020, she founded ASL Picture Books to address the lack of representation of Deaf culture in children's books, and published her award-winning debut children's book, *My Monster Truck Goes Everywhere With Me*. A senior herself, Kathleen is proud to be the project manager for the *Seniors Sign, Too!* series.

Website: https://www.aslpicturebooks.com, Email: info@aslpicturebooks.com,
Social Media: FB, IG @aslpicturebooks

DEBBIE RISH-GREEN

DEBBIE RISH-GREEN is a Los Angeles native and community networker with a B.A. degree in Business Management and two associates degrees. She is the author of *Rocky the Clown*, the executive producer of *Africa In My Veins*, collaborator author of *Marriage Ain't Fa Punks*, and co-project manager, director and co-writer of the *Seniors Sign, Too!* video series. Debbie found her new love for the Deaf community in her role as key production assistant on the *Unheard Voices Season 1* talk show project. She is a certified instructor of English as a Foreign Language (TEFL) and teaches international students online. Debbie is a dedicated wife, mother, and pastor.

Email: rockytheclownfan@gmail.com, Social Media:
Facebook @rockytheclown, IG @thecoolestclown

COMING SOON!

FOLLOW US

SUBSCRIBE TO OUR MAILING LIST

www.signwithme.org

THANK YOU!

CONTACT
Sign with Me, Incorporated

@signwithmeorg
www.signwithme.org
Email: hearzerosales@signwithme.org
Phone: (310) 362-8290
VP (213) 647-3903

*Partial proceeds from sales support ASL education, deaf institutions and organizations.

SUPPORT ACCESSIBLE MEDIA WITH A DONATION TODAY!

SPECIAL THANKS

My sincerest thanks to all those who made this vision manifest.
I love and appreciate you all for your contributions
and believing in our vision!

ASL ALPHABET

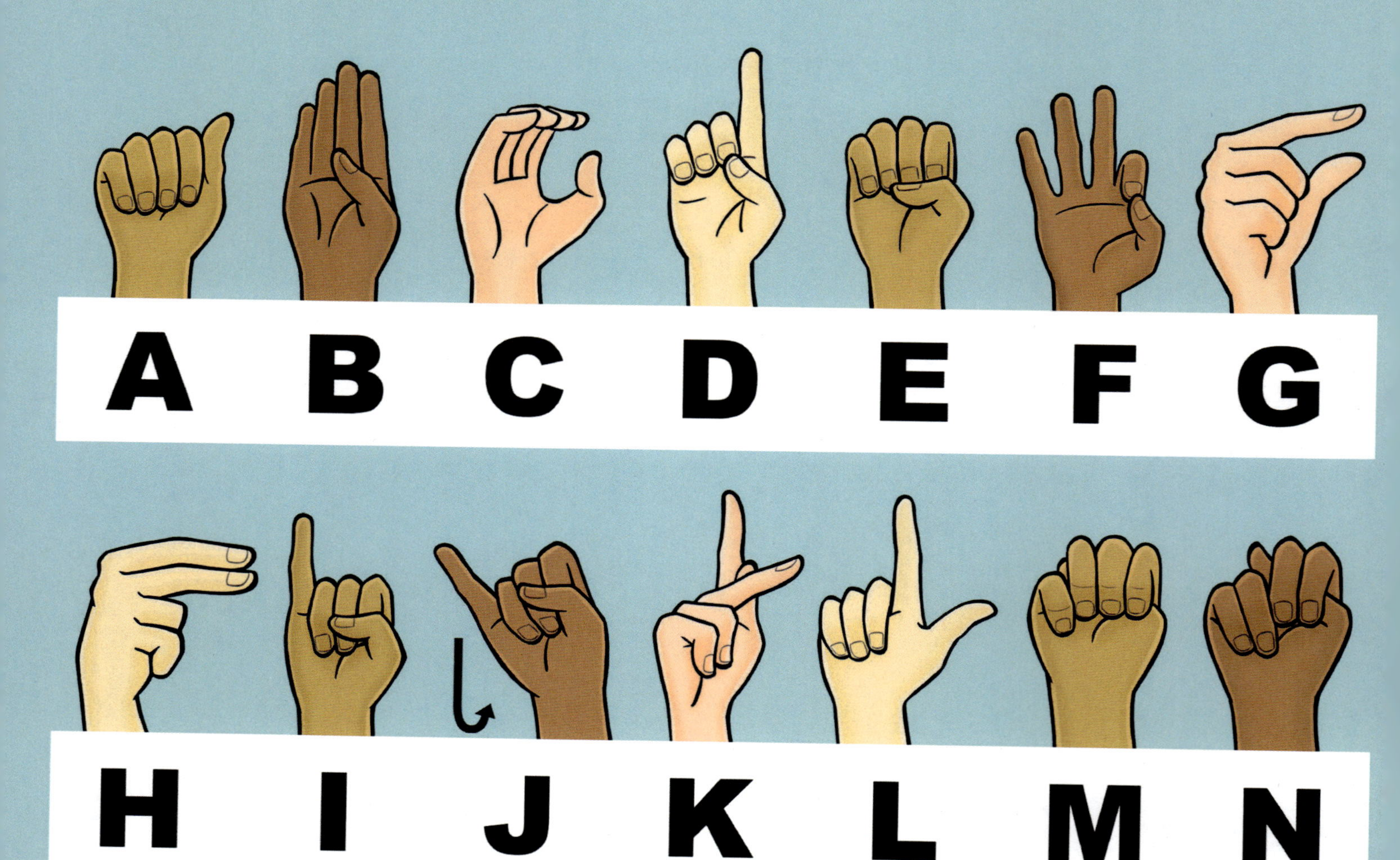

O P Q R S T U

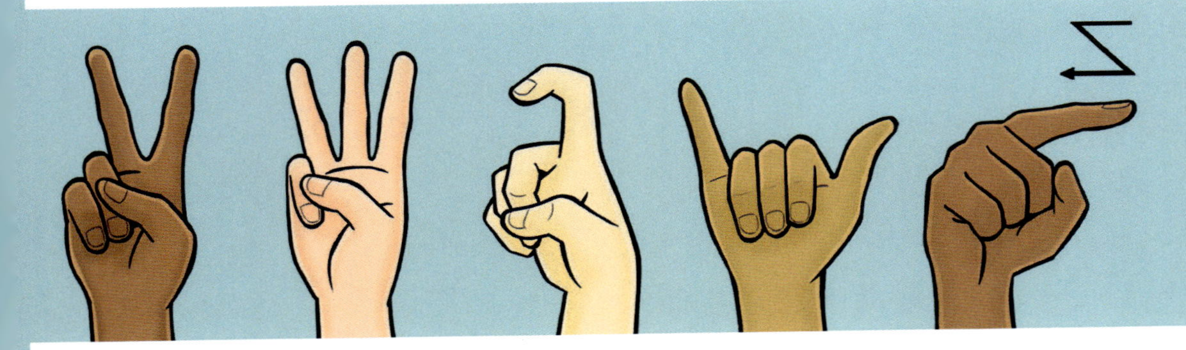

V W X Y Z

MEET THE CHARACTERS

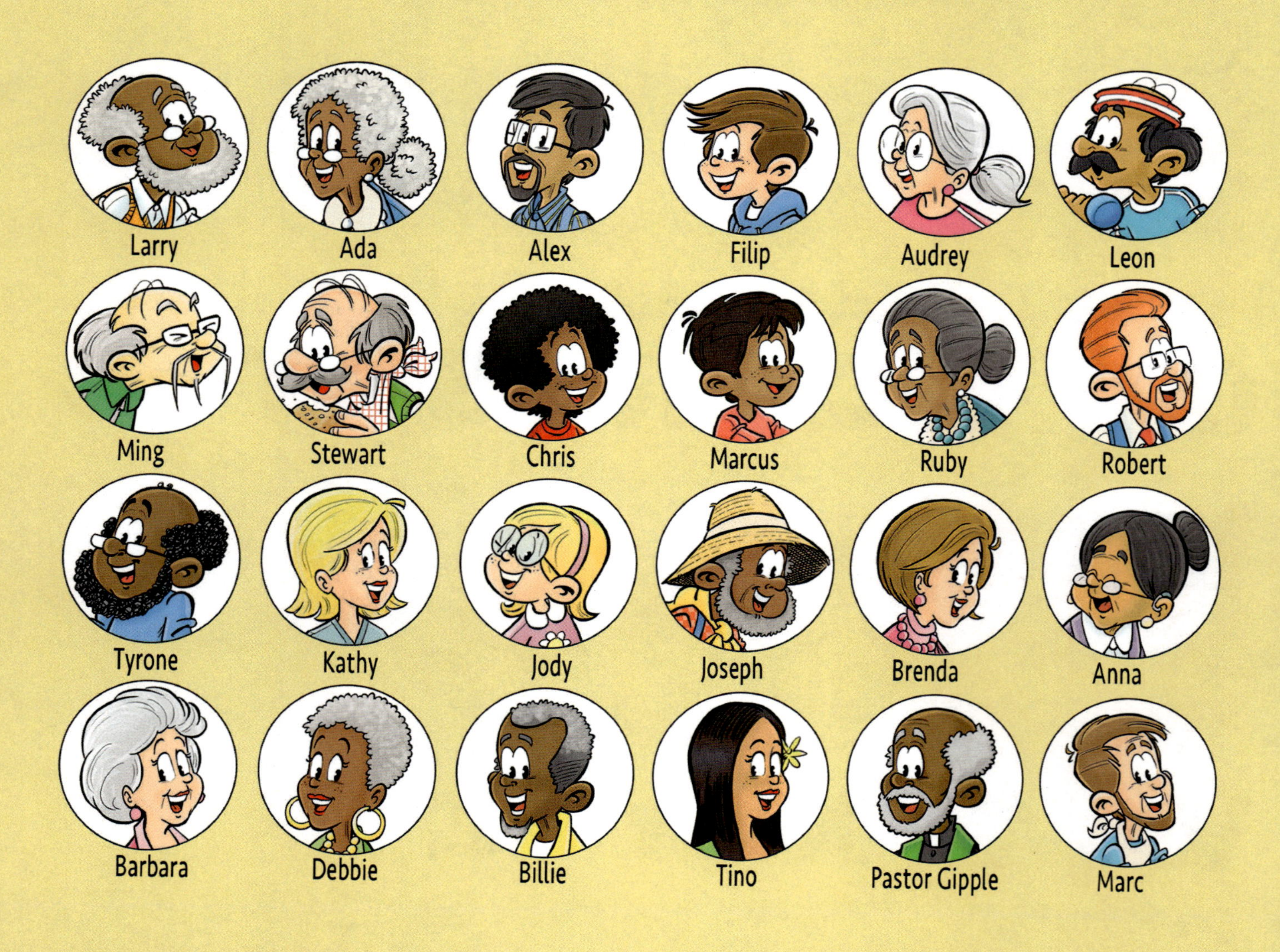

Joyce
Willard
Sharon
Ernie
Enrique
Dennis
Katrien
Heather
Vickie
Milton
Jessie
Dr. Ron
Frank
David
Ramona
Dr. Deven
Cheerio
Meatball

LANGUAGE MODELS

Made in the USA
Columbia, SC
22 November 2022